Dear
Natalie &
Kayla,
Always remember
to be kind & thoughtful
& your days will be sunshine.
Good luck,
Peggy Newfield

June 2015

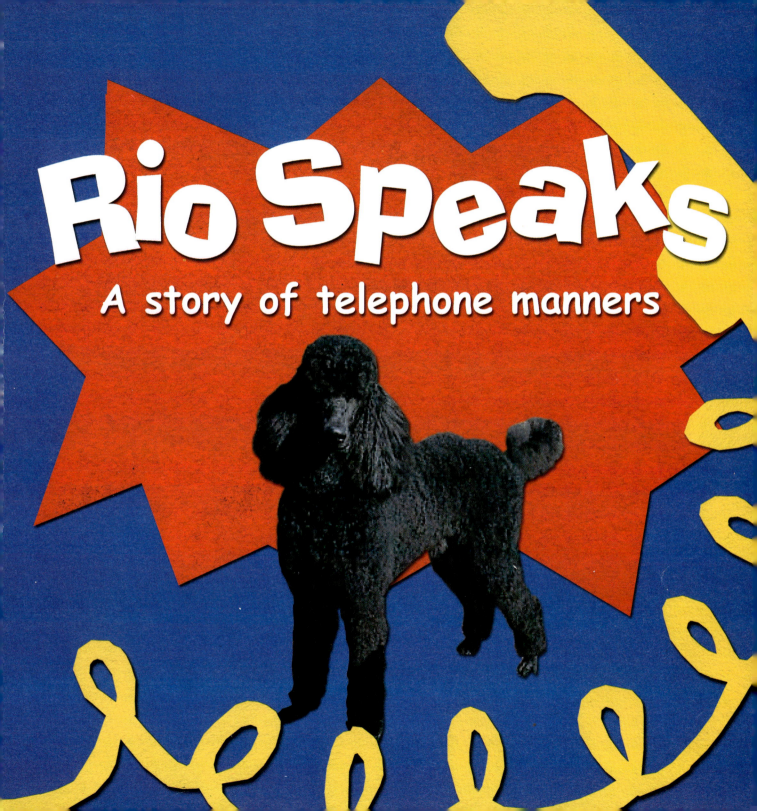

Rio Speaks

A story of telephone manners

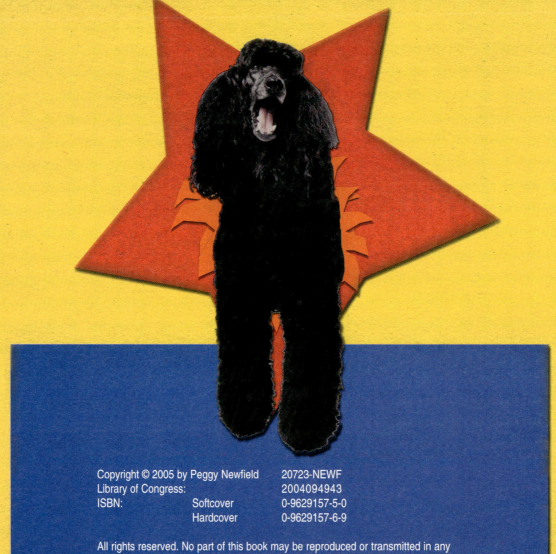

This story is based on actual events. The author, to preserve their anonymity, has
changed names of characters and places. This book is printed in the United States
of America.

To order additional copies of this book, contact:
    Xlibris Corporation   Personal Best, Inc.
    1-888-795-4274   404-252-2245
    www.Xlibris.com   www.personalbest.net
    orders@xlibris.com

A Note from the Author about
Rio!

If you are very lucky, sometime in your life, you may have a pet that is so intelligent and loving that it seems to know all of your thoughts before you speak.

For our family, Rio, our standard poodle, is that special animal.

Over 10,000 children have come to "etiquette" classes in our home, and Rio has greeted each student personally. He is exceptionally polite, very neat when he dines, and always uses perfect manners.

Rio and David have many other stories to share with you.

This, Rio's first book, is based on a true story.

Special Thanks
To the following individuals who have played important roles throughout our Rio Series.

Mary Claire Ferachi,
our 8-year old advisor, who assisted with
the development of Rio's first book

Melanie Clark

Michelle Moore

Joanne Truffelman

Lauren Genkinger

Michael Winner

Cathy Zielinski

Norma Hunt

Our dedicated office staff at
Personal Best, Inc.

Steve Newfield,
my husband and friend,
who listened attentively to ideas,
story lines and rewrites.

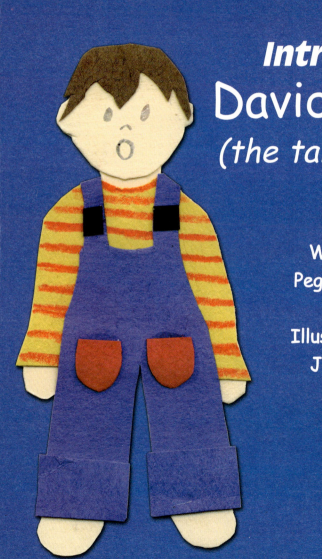

Introducing
David and Rio
(the talking poodle)

Written by:
Peggy Newfield

Illustrations by:
Julie Hagan

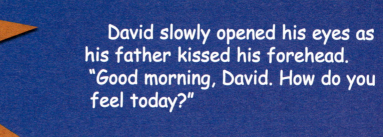

David slowly opened his eyes as his father kissed his forehead. "Good morning, David. How do you feel today?"

David gave a weak smile, happy to see his father's face. Then he coughed a horrible sounding cough. With a frown on her face, his mother poked her head in the door.

"That sounded terrible!" Mrs. Smith said. She came over and sat down on the bed beside her son and gave him a gentle hug.

"So, how are you feeling today?" she asked.

"Okay, I guess," David replied, and then coughed once again.

The fever was gone, but with that yucky sounding cough, David's parents agreed that he should stay home from school again today.

His mother gave him a little squeeze and a kiss and went downstairs to prepare breakfast.

"I'm sure Rio will be happy that you are staying home one more day," Mr. Smith said as he was leaving.

David snuggled back down under his warm covers. He heard his dog, Rio, trotting up the stairs toward his bedroom.

Rio had pure black hair that was very soft, styled in a perfect poodle cut, and big, round, brown eyes.

Rio was a very special dog. . . quite. . . extraordinary. . . even. . . magical, you might say. . . because,

Rio, the exceptionally well-mannered poodle,

could talk!

This was a secret that only he and David shared.

Wagging his puffball tail, the black poodle came over and placed his front paws up on the side of the bed covers.

"Good morning, David," Rio said in his most polite poodle voice. "I hope you are feeling better today."

Sitting up in bed, David stretched. "Yes, I do feel a little better today, thank you," he said as he scratched Rio behind his ears.

"David, your breakfast is ready," his mother called out.

With Rio by his side, David got out of bed and went downstairs.

After breakfast, David was feeling better, so he decided to do some of his homework. Last week's subject was "Telephone Manners."

Getting comfortable in bed, with Rio close by, he took out all of his folders and notes and began looking over his assignment.

Rio stretched up on the side of the bed and saw the long list of things David needed to learn.

"Whew!! I'm glad I don't use the phone. Will you read the list to me?" Rio asked.

Reading from his notes, David began:

Good Telephone Etiquette:

- Always identify who you are when placing a call. . .
"Hi, this is David. May I speak with Paul?"

- Is it too early, or is it too late? Look at the clock before you call. You may have to wait.

- Ask before using someone else's phone. You are a guest in someone else's house, not alone.

- The telephone is not a toy. If you want to play, find a girl or boy.

   ". . . Or a dog!" Rio added. David laughed.

- Listening on the extension is RUDE! Please be polite. Never intrude.

- It's hard to remember every name, number and word.
  Write down each message, exactly what you heard.

- Speak slowly. Speak clearly. Speak as clearly as you can.
  It helps the other person to better understand.

- Prepare a nice greeting when you answer the phone, like. . . "Smith residence. . . David speaking. . ." in your most polite tone.

- Turn off your cell phone before a performance starts, or the people around you will miss the best parts.

- Don't use a cell phone when you sit down to eat.
  Eating uninterrupted is always a treat!

- Be aware of your surroundings when on your cell phone. Don't be too loud. You may not be alone. Besides intruding on others, invading their space, you must protect your information.
  Just in case.

"I like those," said Rio. "Keep reading, David."

- When the phone rings, if you need to call another person to come, cover the mouthpiece or you'll hurt their eardrum.

- If you need help in an emergency, dial 911. The operator will stay on the phone with you until help comes.

"Oh, that's a really good one to remember," said Rio.

- Apologize if you dialed and made a mistake. Don't just hang up for goodness sake!

- Use a happy sounding voice when speaking on the phone. And, never tell a caller that you are home alone.

Wagging his tail, Rio added, ". . . then be nice to your dog, and give him a bone!"

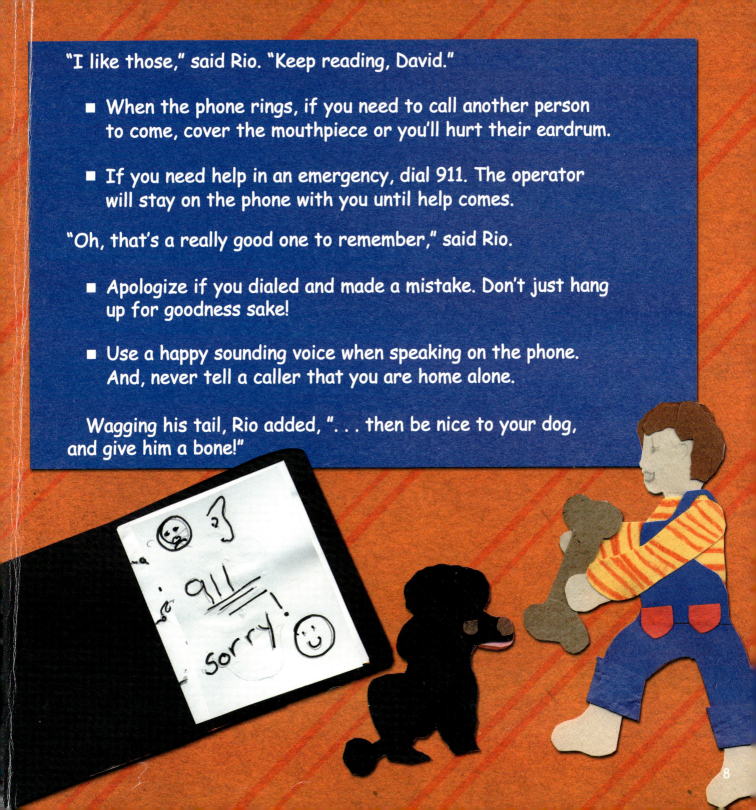

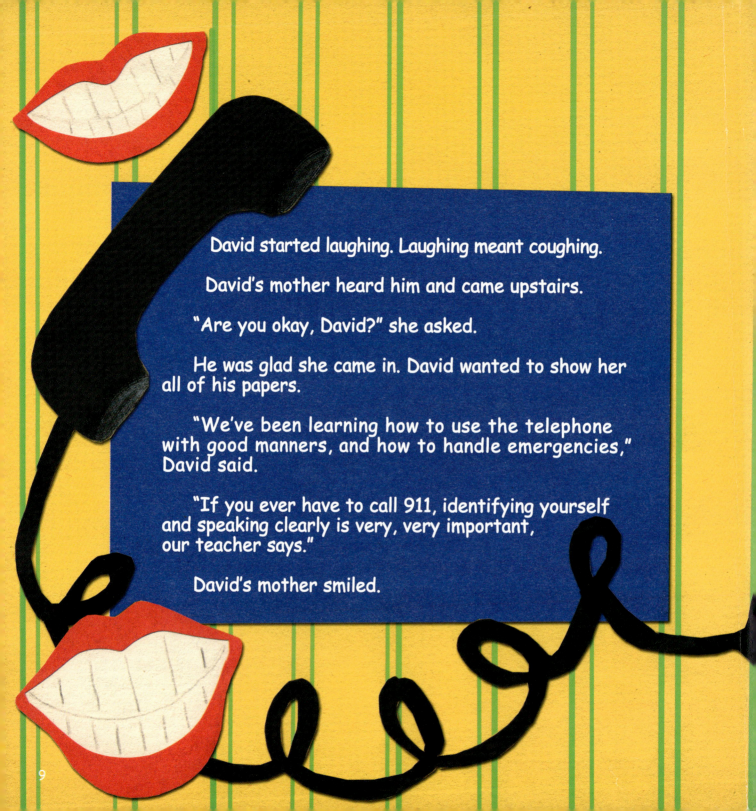

David started laughing. Laughing meant coughing.

David's mother heard him and came upstairs.

"Are you okay, David?" she asked.

He was glad she came in. David wanted to show her all of his papers.

"We've been learning how to use the telephone with good manners, and how to handle emergencies," David said.

"If you ever have to call 911, identifying yourself and speaking clearly is very, very important, our teacher says."

David's mother smiled.

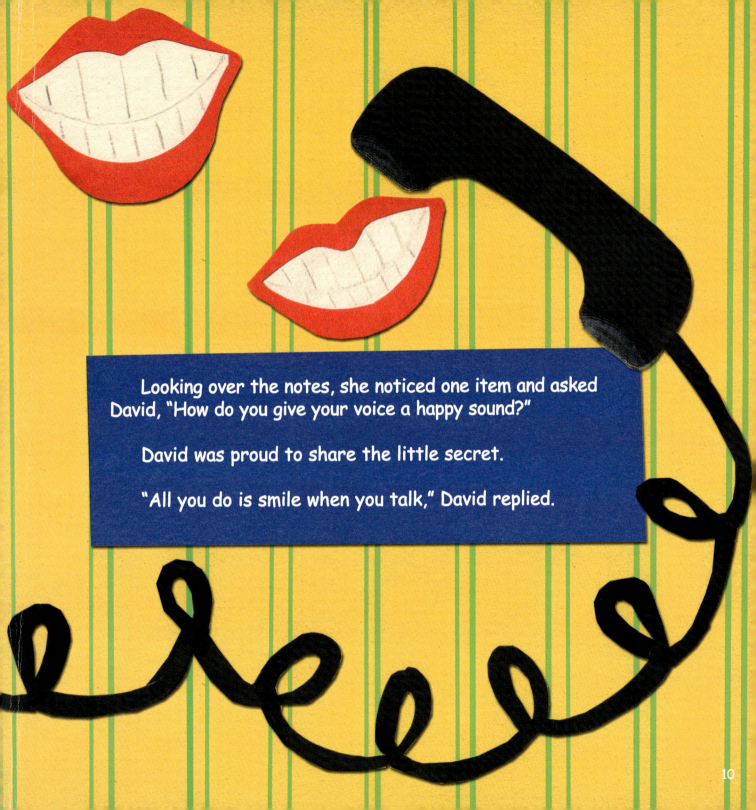

Looking over the notes, she noticed one item and asked David, "How do you give your voice a happy sound?"

David was proud to share the little secret.

"All you do is smile when you talk," David replied.

Mrs. Smith noticed that Rio seemed to be listening so intently to everything David was sharing. "Let's talk to Rio with a happy sounding voice and tell him something that he won't like."

With a big smile on her face and a very happy sounding voice, Mrs. Smith said, "Rio, let's give you a bath and trim your toenails."

Rio jumped up and immediately tried to hide under David's bed.

"Oh!" said a shocked Mrs. Smith. "If I didn't know better, I'd say that Rio understood what I just said."

She got up and patted Rio's back. "I'm sorry Rio. . . I was just kidding. You look beautiful today. Oh. . . what am I saying? He can't understand me!"

Giving her son a kiss on the cheek, Mrs. Smith tousled David's hair. "I'm so proud of all the things you are learning, David. Keep up the good work."

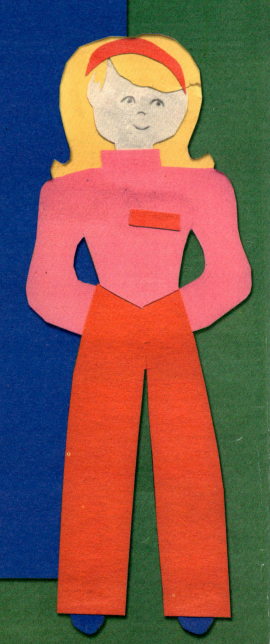

After she left, Rio came out from under the bed and looked up at David.

"Very funny!" said Rio.

All of a sudden, David heard a bang against the wall and his mother yell. Then,

crash! boom!

Someone was falling.

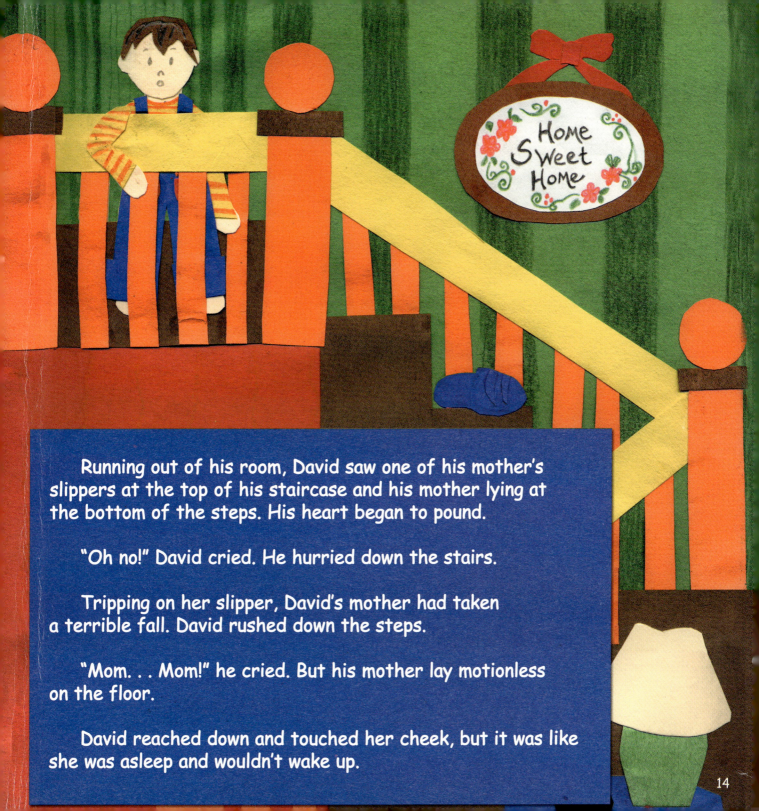

Running out of his room, David saw one of his mother's slippers at the top of his staircase and his mother lying at the bottom of the steps. His heart began to pound.

"Oh no!" David cried. He hurried down the stairs.

Tripping on her slipper, David's mother had taken a terrible fall. David rushed down the steps.

"Mom. . . Mom!" he cried. But his mother lay motionless on the floor.

David reached down and touched her cheek, but it was like she was asleep and wouldn't wake up.

15

Rio was right there beside David.

"Stay calm, David," Rio said. "Don't panic. Your Mom really needs you. Remember your homework this week, what to do in case of an emergency?" Rio asked in his calmest voice.

David's heart was pounding!

Rio nudged David's leg. "David! What should you do?" Rio asked.

"Call for help," David said, as he tried to hold back tears.

David's hands were shaking as he picked up the telephone.

Then David remembered the words from class. . .

"If you need help in an emergency, dial 911. . . speak slowly and clearly."

"911 emergency, how can I help you?" David's voice was quivering.

"This is David Smith. I live at 103 Windsong Lane and my mother is hurt."

"Please tell me exactly what is wrong," said the operator.

Rio rubbed against David again to let him know that he was right there with him. "Calmly, David," Rio reminded him.

David took a deep breath and replied, "She fell down the stairs and she's not moving. Can you please help?"

"Yes, David." The voice assured him. "I have just sent an ambulance to your house. It's on the way."

"Do you have a big blanket?" the operator asked.

"Yes," answered David.

"Please get it and cover your mother. This will keep her warm. I'll wait on the phone for you," she assured him.

David dashed to the closet, pulled out a blanket and began to cover his mother. Rio grabbed a section of the blanket with his teeth and pulled it down over Mrs. Smith's feet.

Grabbing the phone again, David said, "I covered her with a blanket."

"Okay. Is she bleeding, David?"

"No, she looks like she is sleeping," David told the operator.

The operator stayed on the phone with David. She told him that when terrible things happen, it seems like a long time before help comes, but it is actually just a few minutes.

Even though David heard her calm words, his heart was still pounding and his hands were still shaking.

David could hear the siren off in the distance. It was getting louder and louder. Then, with a huge sigh of relief, he told the operator the ambulance had arrived.

"You are a very brave young man, David. You've done a great job," she said.

David slowly opened the door and peeked out as the ambulance pulled into the driveway. The driver and his assistant quickly came up to the door and asked David if they could see his mother.

David let them in.

"Is she going to be all right?" David asked, fighting back tears.

"Yes, your Mom bumped her head pretty hard when she fell, but she's going to be just fine."

David didn't really hear what the men were saying. Staring at his mother, he reached out, and touched her cheek.

This time, Mrs. Smith turned her head towards him, opened her eyes and smiled. "What happened?" she asked softly.

The ambulance driver told Mrs. Smith all that had taken place and how her young son called 911 for help.

Mrs. Smith took David's hand and gently squeezed it. "My brave boy. . ." she whispered. "I love you."

Hearing the siren Mrs. MacDonald, the next-door neighbor, rushed over to see if she could help. Giving David a comforting hug, she insisted on staying at David's house until Mr. Smith came home.

WINDSONG LANE

David went upstairs to his room, with Rio following right behind him. All the commotion that had taken place in the last 30 minutes was just too much. David burst into tears.

Rio put his head in David's lap and looked up at him with those big round poodle eyes.

David couldn't stop crying. He held Rio tightly around his neck and said, "I couldn't have done this without you, Rio." David squeezed even harder.

The poodle started gasping for breath.

"Oh. . . well. . . thanks. . . David. . . but. . . could. . . you. . . lighten up. . . a little?

I can't. . . breathe. . .!"

"Oh, sorry Rio, are you okay?" David asked, wiping away his tears.

Rio cocked his head and looked up at David. "Accidents are always scary, but you did a great job. You remembered everything you have been learning in class. You should be very proud of yourself."

David hugged Rio once again.

Mrs. Smith was going to be just fine despite a big bump on her head. The news spread quickly, and that evening when David's father brought her home from the hospital, the local newspaper was there waiting for them. David had never seen so many cameras before, all flashing at one time. But the surprising thing was that the reporters seemed to be more interested in him than in his mother.

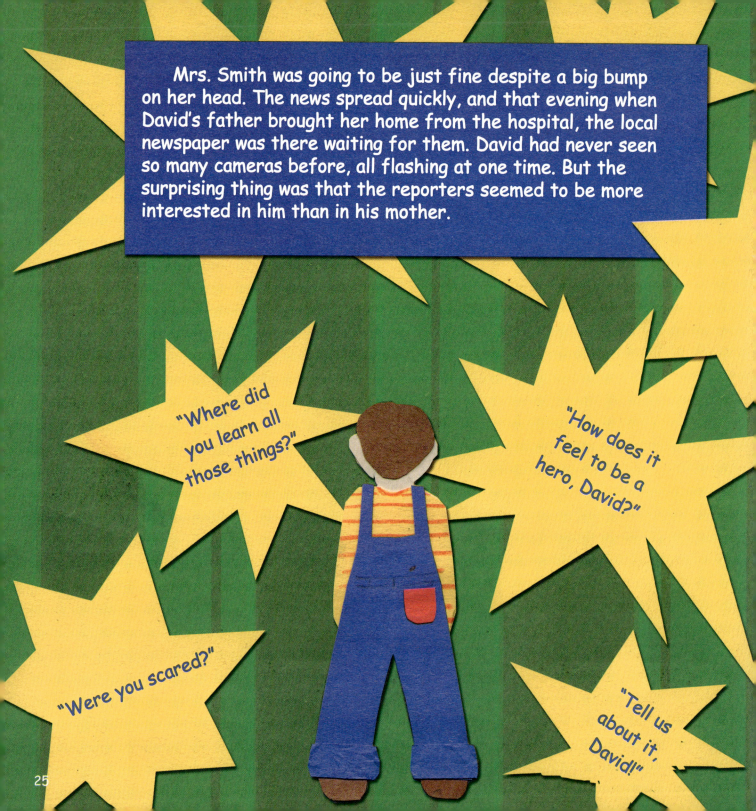

Instead of answering any of their questions, David just ran to his mother and hugged her.

She hugged him back and whispered in his ear, "You're my hero. I love you."

BRAVE BOY SAVES MOTHER

The next day, the local newspaper ran a picture of David on the front page. Under the picture was the story of his brave actions and calm thinking that helped his mother.

David and his mother were given the opportunity to meet the 911 operator. She came over to him and placed a gold medal around his neck. Again all the cameras flashed. It was like the fourth of July.

The medal was so beautiful. . . all shiny and engraved.

PRESENTED TO
DAVID SMITH
FOR
BRAVERY

David felt so proud.

At school the next day, David had something very exciting for "Show and Tell."

PRESENTED TO
DAVID SMITH
FOR
BRAVERY

Rio wants to hear from you!

All letters and e-mails are answered, so write to Rio at:

735 Langford Lane
Atlanta, Georgia 30327

or e-mail him at:

Rio@personalbest.net

Be kind to all animals. They have feelings, too. Feed them, exercise them, and love them, and they will be your best friends!